BEING**THERE**

STANLEY REILLY

Published in 2003 by:
Waverley Care
58a Queen Street
Edinburgh EH2 3NS
Telephone: 0131 226 2206
Facsimile: 0131 226 2209
email: fund@waverleycare.org

in association with
Gray's School of Art
Garthdee Road
Aberdeen AB10 7QD
Telephone: 01224 263600
Facsimile: 01224 263636
email: grays@rgu.ac.uk

Photography:
Stanley Reilly © 2003

Design:
Ian Cargill © 2003

Captions and Introduction:
Richard Mowe © 2003

ISBN 0-9544729-0-X

Printed in Scotland by Inglis:Allen, Kirkcaldy, Fife.

STANLEY REILLY

The relationship between celebrity photographer and subject was not always so hostile and cut-throat as it appears today. Compared to the harsh and frenetic 1980s and 90s during which the cult of personality had become big business, the two preceding decades seem like an age of innocence.

That quality of unsullied harmony and a sense of wonder pervades the photographs of Stanley Reilly who ventured forth from his unlikely Edinburgh background into a London whirl of seemingly continuous first nights, premières and glamorous occasions attended by the rich, famous and a smattering of obligatory wannabes.

Now 60, Stanley accumulated a treasure trove of portraits which capture the exhilarating tempo of the times. Perhaps only with hindsight can their true value and unique perspective be appreciated.

Certainly at the time Stanley was too engrossed in his new found world while trying to keep together his body and soul, to reflect on the intrinsic value and durability of the pictures he was taking with his trusty Pentax, still an inseparable ally.

His natural reserve, born of an Edinburgh childhood and youth as an orphan growing up in care, left him without any inbuilt self-confidence. He was further disadvantaged by dyslexia which hampered his conventional education and progress. He was restless and in and out of jobs every few months until he made a momentous decision to start afresh. All the friends he had known in his formative years had found jobs elsewhere or had decided to move away. He opted for London although he had no contacts or points of reference.

"I hesitated because it was a confusing time. I wanted a new beginning, but I couldn't be sure it was the right thing. I was scared about what was going to happen to my life," he says. "When I first arrived in London I slept rough for six months until I found a flat in Tufnell Park. I worked as a building site labourer." Although his passion for photography was yet to bloom he had been given a Box Brownie by the staff in one of the homes which provided him with a photographic record of his childhood and adolescence. He treasures the results even today.

He became conscious that London was the centre of the entertainment universe. Premières, glamour and excitement, relayed on television to his modest abode, were happening - and it all appeared to be going on just down the road. He had this strange compulsion to satiate his curiosity. He began hanging out with the crowds in Leicester Square, rubbing shoulders with complete strangers under neon-lit canopies. He was drawn inexorably to the photographers waiting at the front of the crush barriers, flash bulbs primed. In turn they were intrigued by the quiet-spoken and polite Scotsman who infiltrated their midst.

Stanley Reilly had arrived. He was leading a double life. By day Jekyll Reilly worked as a labourer and did other menial jobs. By night Hyde Reilly hit the bright lights of the West End. His sense of satisfaction came from taking the pictures, the companionship and playing his role in the whole panoply of events, now part of history.

Stanley Reilly in the Seventies, aged 35, through the lens of a friend.

FOREWORD: Sir Elton John

BEING**THERE** is a celebration. Not only does it capture a wealth of talent during an exciting and fast-paced period of our past, but it also celebrates achievement; the achievement of one man over his own difficulties and the ability of an organisation to give people back their confidence and self-esteem.

Stanley Reilly's story will inspire even the hardest of hearts. His enthusiasm for his hobby and determination to meet and photograph the stars of 1960s and 1970s London has resulted in an impressive personal collection. Unable to compete in a competitive market due to his severe dyslexia, Stanley was undeterred and this publication now demonstrates the extent of his talent.

Stanley has asked that all royalties on the sale of BEING**THERE** should be donated to Waverley Care, Scotland's largest HIV charity, with whom he has been volunteering for the past seven years. He believes that being a café volunteer has given him the confidence to look ahead with optimism and, through publishing this book, he shares this optimism with us.

I am particularly pleased that Waverley Care will benefit from the book. My own Foundation, the Elton John AIDS Foundation, has been pleased to give funding to Waverley Care for many years, directly enabling them to support hundreds of individuals whose lives have been touched by HIV or AIDS. Stanley's work as a volunteer has played an important part in this process and I am glad that, indirectly, we have also been able to help him.

Enjoy!

Elton John all decked out in fur jacket, high heels, silk trousers and his own tee-shirt for a Royal Command Performance in October 1972.
Stanley recalls that "he was a bit nervous about going on. This was taken during a break in rehearsals."

Elton – by command

A fashion model arrives for a London première in
1971 and immediately starts a bulb-popping
frenzy. The film was The Last Valley with Michael
Caine and Omar Sharif.

"We all looked smart with collars and ties.
Nowadays it's more informal," says Stanley.

The first Lady of Brit -pop

Dusty Springfield in 1968, attending a charity show at the Palladium
where other guests included comedian Norman Wisdom and horror star
Christopher Lee. This was the only photo Stanley took on that
occasion as he didn't like to impose.

Anita Harris, the singer, with her pooch as she
leaves the London Palladium after rehearsals for a
1968 Royal Variety Show. Stanley timed it perfectly.

"She was just going as I arrived," he recalls.

Barbara Windsor was always a willing first-nighter: here she arrives for a screening of Sunflower with Sophia Loren and Marcello Mastroianni at Leicester Square Theatre (now the Odeon West End).

"I photographed her quite a lot at different places including Pinewood studios for the Carry On films."

Funny Girl Babs

Ginger Rogers crossed the Atlantic for a charity event
in the Theatre Royal, Drury Lane in 1971.

" I managed to get there just as she was arriving. It
was pouring rain but this was too good an opportunity
to miss – catching a Hollywood legend."

Dancing Queen

Judy Garland arrives late at the London Palladium in 1969. Stanley waited on long after the other photographers had left. His persistence brought dividends. This photograph was taken during the last few months of Garland's life.

"It was obvious she was suffering - and she was almost dragged into the theatre," says Stanley.

Final Curtain

Zsa Zsa Gabor in her finery for the première of Sean Connery's first Western Shalako, in which he co-starred with Brigitte Bardot. Zsa Zsa was an indispensable component of the celebrity circuit of the Sixties and Seventies.

"She was always a bit over the top but the photographers loved her."

Cleo Laine at the London Palladium in November 1972. She
was rehearsing for a Royal Variety Show. Stanley was allowed to
shoot from his favourite place in the wings.

Singing for her supper

Horror film actress **Ingrid Pitt** arrives for the première of Camelot at the Odeon in Leicester Square in 1970.

"She was the epitome of Sixties' glamour," says Stanley.

Horror queen

Jilly Johnson was one of the super models of the Seventies who had standing invitations to add a dash of spice to first nights and screenings. The dress was the equivalent of Liz Hurley's safety pin number for its scale of daring.

Shirley Bassey struts her stuff at the London Palladium in November 1971 before an audience which included Princess Anne. Stanley had a vantage point in the front row.

Celebrities' Sign

Liz Taylor and **Richard Burton** at the Round House theatre
in North London for an October 1970 charity auction of
posters and photographs. She was proudly showing off her
£1 million diamond wedding ring. Stanley was one of only
two lensmen in attendance.

A sparkling pair

Sean Connery and **Diane Cilento,** mother of Jason, attend the first night of Connery's Western Shalako which co-starred Brigitte Bardot. Sir Sean always recognised Stanley as a fellow son of Auld Reekie.

Professional Cockney **Michael Caine** with his wife
Shakira stepping out for a West End film première
in 1971. Stanley caught up with him decades later
when he came to Festival Edinburgh for the
screening of a restored print of The Man Who Would
Be King with Sean Connery.

Togetherness

TV celebrity **David Frost** and **Diahann Caroll,**
the American actress, attend the launch of
Hal Wallis's film of Mary Queen of Scots with
Vanessa Redgrave and Glenda Jackson at the
Odeon Leicester Square in March 1972.

Michael York and his wife Pat McCallum, who's a photographer. They were stepping out as a glamorous couple for a Sixties film première.

Disc jockey **Tony Blackburn**, who began in
the Sixties on pirate radio, partnered by
Lynne Partington for a West End event.

Telly Savalas, forever Kojak, joined the throng with a
friend for the world première of The Magic Christian.
With his grinning demeanour and Greek parentage he
became one of showbiz's most famous baldies.

Tough guy

Ringo and his girlfriend turn out at the
Odeon in Kensington in 1969 for the
unveiling of The Magic Christian in which
he was paired with Peter Sellers.

John Lennon and Yoko
Ono sally forth for the
première of The Magic
Christian featuring Ringo
Starr in December 1969 at
the Odeon in Kensington.

"There was a crowd
outside and I heard they
were arriving. I just
waited there and they
stood and posed. I
thought he might have
been a lookalike but he
was the real thing."

Lennon - for real

Michael "Parky" Parkinson and his wife Mary
at the première of 10 Rillington Place in 1971
at the Columbia Cinema in Shaftesbury Avenue.

Topol and his wife attend the première of Fiddler on
the Roof at the Plaza and run the gauntlet of some
protests about Russian anti-semitism.

Ken Dodd wisecracks his way around the London Palladium in 1972 as he awaits his turn at a Royal Variety Show which was also attended by the likes of Mike Yarwood, Rod Hull and Emu, Elton John and Dickie Henderson.

Dudley Moore joins the throng for a Pink Panther moment in London's West End. He was rubbing shoulders with Peter Sellers, Omar Sharif, Lulu, Twiggy, Lionel Blair, Simon Dee and Pete Murray and his wife.

"It was one of those nights with so many celebrities that I wish I'd had 20 arms," says Stanley.

Cuddly Dudley

Frankie Vaughan was besieged by fans as he was making his escape from the stage door of the London Palladium where he had been performing in his own one-man show in 1968.

"Actually I did not know much about him, except I knew he was mega-big at the time."

Fans for Frankie

Anthony Quayle at Speakers' Corner who just happened to be there with his son, proudly displays one of the first Polaroid cameras. Stanley was intrigued - and the pair became engrossed in conversation.

Conversation piece

Danny La Rue was one of a cast of hundreds
who could not wait to sample the peace and
love of the groundbreaking musical Hair when
it opened in the West End in 1969.

Liberace was always the centre of attention
whether he was performing or simply attending.
The king of kitsch was preparing to settle down for
an evening's enjoyment in the audience of a West
End show in 1970.

Prince of glam

John Hurt made one of his early screen forays in
10 Rillington Place, about the notorious Christie
murders of the Forties. Hurt was attending the
film's première in 1971.

Eric Sykes, who like many comics of his generation was
introduced to showbusiness while in the Army, produced
scripts for Bill Fraser, Frankie Howerd, Peter Sellers and
Stanley Unwin, as well as appearing himself.

Sid James and **Dora Bryan**, (part of the Carry On
crew) were among the celebrities at the Odeon,
Leicester Square, for the Royal Film Performance in
1971 of Little Big Man.

Carry on sparkling

Dustin Hoffman in town in April 1971 for the
London première of Arthur Penn's Western
Little Big Man.

"He was waiting for the chauffeur to pick him
up after the screening and he smiled at me as
I took the picture."

Tales of Hoffman

Lee Marvin at the Astoria in London's Tottenham
Court Road for the première of the musical Paint
Your Wagon.

Stanley recalls that the star "was very amenable" as
he lined up to meet Princess Anne.

Roger (The Saint) Moore out on the town in his
pre-007 days. Stanley established a relaxed rapport
with Moore who was always happy to greet him.

David Hemmings, the star of one of Stanley's favourite films Blow Up which was all about photography, and a lot of it filmed in King's Road. Hemmings (and his then wife actress Gayle Hunnicutt) appeared in matching high collar jackets for a London film première. This was the only chance Stanley had of photographing the elusive Hemmings.

Snap happy

RRITAIN

John Lennon used the première of The Magic Christian to voice
concerns about the case of convicted A6 murderer James Hanratty
who was hung for a murder he said he did not commit. Lennon and
others, holding a placard stating "Britain Murdered Hanratty", were
arguing for the case to be reopened.

Protest in profile

Sir Cliff Richard performs at a huge outdoor
concert in Hyde Park as part of a Festival of
Light rally. The crowd gathered in Trafalgar
Square in September 1971 before marching
to the Park to listen to speeches and songs
with a spiritually uplifting theme.

"I've photographed Cliff several times,
notably when I was invited to his 40th
birthday party," says Stanley.

Sweetness and light

The Jacksons ran the gauntlet of clamouring fans at
Heathrow to make it in time for the Royal Variety
show in October 1972. They lined up at the Palladium
just before going on stage before The Queen.

Harry Secombe appeared out of the blue in Drury Lane. Stanley says he took off his glasses, and pulled one of his stockpile of famously funny faces.

"It was quite an honour because I'd always been a fan."

Spike Milligan relaxes with a drink in the mid-Sixties
at the Round House, London's cutting edge theatre
space which still survives. Stanley joined him...

Clown celebration

Peter Sellers looks resplendent in snakeskin jacket for the Royal Film Performance in January, 1969.

Marty Feldman, the distinctively featured comedian who moved swiftly on from writing to performing and became a huge hit. At the peak of his fame in the Sixties, here he signs an autograph outside the London Palladium in 1969.

An eyeful of Marty

Richard Harris who played King Arthur to
Vanessa Redgrave's Guinevere, cuts a dash at the
London première of Camelot in 1968.

A regal entrance

Omar Sharif was one of the many star guests at 1969's
Royal Film Performance. Besides Sharif and Sellers the
throng included Simon Dee, Lulu and Dudley Moore.

Charlton Heston took on the Bard with his
production of Antony and Cleopatra premièred at
the Dominion in London in 1972. He wrote the
adaptation, directed it, and played Antony to
Hildegarde Neil's Cleopatra.

Hollywood royalty

American comedian **Bob Hope** hosted a
Sixties Miss World contest at the Royal
Albert Hall. He was friendly but the
feminists were not amused about what
they perceived was a "cattle market" and
demeaning to women.

Hope springs ...

Ryan O'Neal, in his Love Story days, was one of the guests at the Royal première of Little Big Man, directed by Arthur Penn.

Lionel Blair, the choreographer, trips the light fantastic at the London Palladium where he was checking out the 1971 Royal Variety Show.

Twinkle toes

Northern Ireland was never far from protest headlines.
A group make their presence felt on the streets of London.

Pointed protest at the 1971 première of Fiddler on the Roof where activists complained about the treatment of Jews in Russia.

Tariq Ali on the march in a rally against the war in Vietnam.
It was the era when protesters regularly took to the streets
to make their views known.

Anti-Vietnam war protesters take it lying down in Hyde Park
in 1968 and are removed by the police.

Protest placards help to vent the anger of the
nuclear disarmament lobby at the traditional
Speakers' Corner in Hyde Park circa 1969.

Placards protesting about the foot and mouth outbreak,
appeared in Hyde Park. The pleas to stop the slaughtering
of cattle have an uncannily familiar ring.

More signs of the times

An unfair cop on the Embankment, as protesters head towards Downing
Street, to voice concerns about immigration and problems over passports.

Against the tide

The banners proclaim: Oppose Red Nazism. The time: the end of the Sixties.
The place: Trafalgar Square, the traditional place of protest.

Neil Armstrong (left) meets the then Prime Minister Harold Wilson outside No. 10 Downing Street in 1969.

"In those days you could get in to the Street without any problem. You wouldn't be able to do that today."

Moon man

The world holds its breath for the safety of the Apollo 13 astronauts.
"You could feel the tension everywhere," says Stanley who believed this
billboard summed up the mood of the times.

An inquisitive face in the crowd tries to get a
reaction out of the immobile and immovable
guardsman at the Trooping of the Colour in 1968.

The Queen Mother leaves the London Palladium with Princess Margaret after enjoying another successful Royal Variety Show in 1969.

A night to remember

The Queen steps out at the Royal première
of The Tales of Beatrix Potter at the ABC (now Odeon Covent Garden) in
Shaftesbury Avenue. In the top right corner is Lord Mountbatten.

On Her Majesty's Service

Prince Charles captured in the Royal Rolls Royce as he attends the première of Chitty Chitty Bang Bang in 1968.

"Unfortunately his car had broken down a 100 yards from the Odeon in Leicester Square. I just happened to see the car, and went over and took the picture through the window. Eventually he and Princess Anne had to get out and walk."

The heir apparent

1   Sir Elton John
2   Fashion Model
3   Dusty Springfield
4   Anita Harris
5   Barbara Windsor
6   Ginger Rogers
7   Judy Garland
8   Zsa Zsa Gabor
9   Cleo Laine
10 Ingrid Pitt
11 Jilly Johnson
12 Shirley Bassey
13 Liz Taylor and Richard Burton
14 Sean Connery and Diane Cilento
15 Michael Caine and Shakira
16 David Frost and Diahann Carol
17 Michael York and Pat McCallum
18 Tony Blackburn and Lynne Partington
19 Telly Savalas
20 Ringo Starr
21 John Lennon and Yoko Ono
22 Michael and Mary Parkinson
23 Topol
24 Ken Dodd
25 Dudley Moore
26 Frankie Vaughan
27 Anthony Quayle
28 Danny La Rue
29 Liberace
30 John Hurt
31 Eric Sykes
32 Sid James and Dora Bryan
33 Dustin Hoffman
34 Lee Marvin
35 Roger Moore
36 David Hemmings
37 John Lennon
38 Sir Cliff Richard
39 The Jacksons
40 Harry Secombe
41 Spike Milligan
42 Peter Sellers
43 Marty Feldman
44 Richard Harris
45 Omar Sharif
46 Charlton Heston
47 Bob Hope
48 Ryan O'Neal
49 Lionel Blair
50 Protest
51 Protest
52 Tariq Ali
53 Anti Vietnam Protest
54 Protest
55 Foot and Mouth
56 Downing Street Protest
57 Trafalgar Square Demonstration
58 Neil Armstrong (left) with Harold Wilson
59 Apollo 13
60 Trooping of the Colour
61 The Queen Mother
62 The Queen
63 Prince Charles
64 The Whisky a GoGo

The club scene was thriving upstairs and downstairs in the
Old Compton Street area in 1966.

Waverley Care and **Stanley Reilly** would like to thank the following individuals and organisations for their part in making this project a reality:

Bank of Scotland
Alex Aikman
Lyndon Antle
Geoff Burrows
Iain Fiddes
Sir Elton John
Elton John AIDS Foundation
Hilary Patrick
Bryce Potter
Kathryn Ross
Jan Rutherford
Paul Scharf
Jeff Simants
Ian Stirling
Gray's School of Art, The Robert Gordon University

Editor
Karen Docwra is a member of Waverley Care's fundraising and development team.

Waverley Care
58a Queen Street
Edinburgh EH2 3NS

Telephone: 0131 226 2206
Facsimile: 0131 226 2209
email: fund@waverleycare.org

Introduction and Scene-setting
Richard Mowe has contributed to national newspapers, radio and television, mainly on cultural affairs and the entertainment and film worlds. He worked for ten years, as arts editor and member of the founding team who established Scotland on Sunday. He is also Director of the French and Italian Film Festivals.

Design and Production
Ian Cargill is a Lecturer at Gray's School of Art in Aberdeen. He is currently the creative director of 50K Design, a professional design consultancy operating in The Robert Gordon University.

Stuart Johnstone is Photographic Application Supervisor at Gray's School of Art in Aberdeen. He has been responsible for printing this selection of negatives from Stanley's collection.

Gray's School of Art, Garthdee Road
Aberdeen AB10 7QD

Telephone: 01224 263612
Facsimile: 01224 263606
email: info@50kdesign.com

Printing
inglis:allen is one of the UK's leading providers of print solutions to the art, design and paper communities.

40 Townsend Place
Kirkcaldy KY1 1HF

Telephone: 01592 267201
Facsimile: 01592 206049
email: jsimants@inglisallen.com

Paper
GF Smith the paper specialists, suppliers of paper to the design and printing industry.

Lockwood Street
Hull HU2 0HL

Telephone: 01482 323 503
Facsimile: 01482 223 174
email: info@gfsmith.com

PAPER:
Cover: Verus Ion 300gsm
Printed in four colours with quadratone photograph
Text: Verus Ion 150gsm
Photographs: Printed in four colours with text in cool grey